SMART BREAD MACHINE

The Complete BREAD MACHINE Cookbook with Lean & Green Meals to Taste, Air Fryer Recipes, The Step-by-Step Weight Loss Program on a Budget

BY

SUSAN GREY

professional before attempting any techniques outlined in this book.

By reading this document, the reader agrees that under no circumstances is the author responsible for any losses, direct or indirect, which are incurred as a result of the use of information contained within this document, including, but not limited to, - errors, omissions, or inaccuracies.

Contents

Introduction

Cooking at home with copycat recipes of your favorite fast food and

restaurant delights has been easier with the number of options available

today. Many of the common meals and featured specials at your local

diners and franchise restaurants can be made at a fraction of the cost and straightforward recipes.

Many restaurants and fast-food outlets today have evolved to include many different flavors from around the world, which gives us a great opportunity to expand the palate and try new meals and options like never before. Scratch cooked recipes are always the greatest. Many people assume, however, that lots of time and product expertise are needed. Many are excluded from cooking and

rely on pre-cooked or drinking meals. Not all products are made in the same way when it comes to healthy options.

Meals in the restaurant can contain several unhealthy ingredients. There is also much more than what you lack when you feed from take-outs. Here are a few explanations why you should consider having your own cooking dinner tonight!

A Nutrient-Dense Plate

If prepared food arrives from outside home; usually, you have limited

knowledge about salt, sugar and processed oils. Actually, we also apply more to our meal when it is served to the table. You will say how much salt, sugar and oil are being used to prepare meals at home.

Portion control from home can also be regulated.

When food is cooked for us, we tend to eat all or most of it. Try to use little dishes at home, but make sure that all good things like vegetables, fruits, whole grains and legumes are filled.

Copycat recipes

Butter Chicken

Planning time: 10 minutesCooking time: 20 minutes; Serving: 6

Fixings

1 ½ pounds chicken bosom, cubed3 teaspoons ground ginger

teaspoons minced garlic2 tablespoons gram masala 1 tablespoon coconut oil ounces almond yogurtFor the Sauce:

1 huge white onion, stripped, quarter2 teaspoons ground ginger

14.5 ounces squashed tomatoes2 teaspoons minced garlic

1 ½ teaspoon salt

1 teaspoon red bean stew powder

tablespoon ground coriander2 teaspoons cumin

½ tablespoon gram masala

tablespoons margarine, unsalted

½ cup weighty creamDirections

Cut the chicken bosom into 2-inch shapes, place them into a huge bowl, add 1 teaspoon every one of ginger and garlic alongside gram masala and yogurt and afterward mix until all around joined.

Spot the chicken into the fridge and let it marinate for at least 30 minutes.

Then, set up the sauce and for this, place onion pieces in the blender, addtomatoes, garlic, ginger, and every one of the flavors and afterward beat for 2 to 3 minutes untilsmooth.

At the point when the chicken has marinated, take an enormous skillet dish, place it over medium-high warmth, add oil and when it liquefies, add marinated chicken pieces and cook for4 minutes for each side until pleasantly sautéed.

At that point pour in the sauce, cook for 6 minutes, add spread and cream and mix until all around blended.

Cook the chicken for another blend, season with salt, and afwaddhnitthedhfrom heat.

Trimming the spread chicken with cilantro and afterward serve.

Nourishment: 293 Cal; 17 g Fats; 29 g Protein; 6 g Net Carb; 3 g Fiber;

Red Lobster's Shrimp Scampi

Cooking time: 10 minutes; Serving: 4

Fixings

¼ pound shrimp, tail eliminated, stripped, de-veined 1 ½ tablespoon minced garlic

scallions, cut

¾ teaspoon salt

½ teaspoon ground dark pepper

¼ teaspoon red pepper drops

¼ cup slashed parsley

4 tablespoons margarine, unsalted

¼ cup lemon juice

¼ cup chardonnay

½ cup destroyed Parmesan chedd Directions

Take an enormous skillet dish, place it over medium warmth, add margarine and when it dissolves, add garlic and cook for 1 moment until delicate and brilliant earthy colored.

Add shrimps, cook them for 3 to 4 minutes until base becomes pink, at that point flip the shrimps by utilizing utensils, sprinkle with red pepper pieces, and keep cooking for 3 minutes.

At that point sprinkle wine and lemon juice over shrimps, cook one more moment and afterward eliminate the container from heat.

Sprinkle scallions and parsley over the shrimps, season with salt and dark pepper, and afterward top with cheddar.

Serve straight away.

Nourishment: 332 Cal; 17 g Fats; 34 g Protein; 7 g Net Carb; 1 g Fiber;

Parmesan Pork Chops

Cooking time: 10 minutes; Serving: 2

Fixings

4 pork slashes, boneless

½ teaspoon garlic powder

¼ teaspoon salt

¼ teaspoon ground white pepper2 tablespoons avocado oil

1 egg

4 ounces destroyed parmesan chedd Directions

Take a little bowl, place garlic powder in it, add salt and dark pepper, and afterward mix until blended.

Sprinkle the zing mix on the two sides of the pork slashes and after that press into it. Take a shallow dish, break the egg in it and after that beat until frothy. Take a secluded shallow dish, put parmesan cheddar on it. Plunge every pork hack into theegg and after that coat with cheddar.

Take a skillet, place it over medium-high warmth, add oil and when hot, add apre-arranged pork slash in it and afterward cook for 5 minutes for each side until carmelized and delicate.

When done, move pork cleaves to a plate and afterward rehash with the leftover slashes.

Serve straight away with cauliflower

pound.

Nourishment: 370 Cal; 26 g Fats; 32 g Protein; 1 g Net Carb; 0 g Fiber;

Buffalo Wild Wings Grilled Chicken Wraps

Cooking Time: 15 minutes Servings: 4

Ingredients

1 lb. boneless skinless chicken breasts2 teaspoons vegetable oil

1 cup KRAFT Mexican Style cheese, shredded1 tomato, chopped

tablespoons KRAFT Zesty Italian Dressing2 teaspoons chili powder

(8") flour tortillaDirections

Heat grill to medium heat;

Coat chicken with oil and then grill for approximately 8 minutes per side or untildone (165ºF); cool slightly;

Spoon down centers of tortillas. Fold in opposing sides of tortillas, then roll upburrito style;

Place, seam sides down, on the grill grate. Grill 4-5 minutes per side or untilevenly browned.

Nutrition: Calorie: 570 kcal Fat: 57 g Carbohydrates: 22 g Sodium: 1560 mg

Protein: 4 g

Buffalo Wild Wings Boneless Wings

Cooking Time: 40 minutes Servings: 4

Ingredients

Cooking Oil for deep frying

1 ⅓ cups unbleached flour, all-purpose2 ¾ teaspoons salt

¾ teaspoon black pepper, ground

¾ teaspoon cayenne pepper

¼ teaspoon garlic powder, granulated

¾ teaspoon paprika 1 ¼ egg

1 ⅓ cups milk

⅓ cup hot pepper sauce

1 tablespoon 1 teaspoon butterDirection

Add and preheat oil in a large-sized saucepan or a deep fryer to 375° F;

Combine paprika, garlic powder, cayenne pepper, salt, black pepper, and flour ina big bowl;

Whisk together the egg as well as milk in a clean small bowl;

Dip each piece of chicken in the egg mixture and then roll in the flour blend.Repeat so that each slice of chicken is double-coated;

Refrigerate breaded chicken for twenty minutes;

Fry the chicken in batches in the hot oil. Cook until the outside is nicelybrowned, as well as the juices run clear, 5 to 6 minutes a batch;

Combine sauce that is hot as well as butter in a clean small bowl;

Microwave sauce on High until melted, 5-6 seconds;Pour sauce over the prepared chicken;

Mix to coat.

Nutrition: Calories: 850 kcal Fat: 52 g Carbohydrates: 58 g Sodium: 2430 mg

Protein: 37 g

KFC Vegan Popcorn Chicken

Cooking Time: 25 Minutes Servings: 3-4 (2 cups)

Ingredients

Dried chunks of soy (2 cups)Grated ginger (1-inch cube)Minced garlic (2 cloves) Flour (.5 cup)

Salt (1 tsp. /as required)Cornstarch (.5 cup)

Vegetable broth - divided (3 cups + .75 cup) Breadcrumbs (1 cup)

Garlic powder (1 tbsp.)Salt (.5 tsp.)

Lemon pepper (1 tbsp.)For the dip:

Soy sour cream (.33 cup) Freshly chopped dill (1

tbsp.)Pepper (dash)

Directions

Combine the chunks of soy, garlic, ginger, and salt in a bowl. Cover the chunksof soy using vegetable broth. Soak until the pieces are soft (20 minutes).

Warm a pot with oil (1-inch) using a med-high temperature setting.

Whisk the flour and vegetable broth from the soaking soy chunks until the lumpsare removed. Add to the two bowls.

Transfer the chunks to a zipper-type bag with the cornstarch. Shake until coated. Toss into the second bowl of flour mixture and coat. Lastly, transfer to another zipper bag that has the breadcrumbs, garlic powder, salt, and lemon pepper.

Fry in batches until golden. Drain on a layer of paper towels.

Blend the sour cream, salt, pepper, and dill in a food processor to prepare the dip.

Nutrition: Calorie: 226 g Fat: 0 g Carbohydrates: 37.75 Sodium: 1861 mg

Protein: 11.2 g

P.F. Chang's™ Vegetarian Lettuce Wraps

Cooking Time: 5 Minutes Servings: 4

Ingredients

Rice vinegar (2 tbsp.)Hoisin sauce (3 tbsp.)Sesame oil (1 tsp.)

Canola oil — or grapeseed oil (2 tsp.)Reduced-sodium soy sauce (3 tbsp.)

Extra-firm tofu - do not use silken (12-14 oz. pkg.) Baby Bella cremini mushrooms (8 oz. - finely chopped)Water chestnuts (8 oz. can) drained and finely chopped Garlic (2 minced cloves)

Freshly grated ginger (2 tsp.) Optional: Red pepper flakes (.25 tsp.)

Green onions (4 thinly sliced - divided)Large inner leaves romaine lettuce (8)

Optional for Serving: Grated carrots + red pepper flakesDirections

Whisk the rice vinegar, soy sauce, hoisin, and sesame oil. Set aside.

Prepare the tofu by pressing it between layers of paper towels while you start thepreparation.

Warm the oil in a large skillet using the med-high temperature setting.

Break the tofu into small pieces and cook for five minutes before adding thediced mushrooms. Simmer until the tofu starts to turn golden (approx. 3 min.).

Stir in the ginger, pepper flakes, water chestnuts, garlic, and half of the onions;simmer for another 30 seconds.

Stir in the sauce and simmer until the sauce is warmed through (30-60 seconds).

Serve the tofu mixture into individual leaves of lettuce. Garnish using the rest ofthe carrots, pepper flakes, and onions before serving.

Nutrition: Calorie: 640 g Fat: 29 g Carbohydrates: 68 g Sodium: 2060 mg

Protein: 24 g

Wendy's™ Spicy Chicken Sandwich – Vegan

Cooking Time: 20 Minutes Servings: 3

Ingredients

Bob's Red Mill gluten-free all-purpose flour (1 cup)Sea salt (1 tbsp.)

Onion powder (1 tsp.)Garlic powder (1 tsp.) Paprika (.5 tsp.) Black pepper (1 tsp.) Tempeh (1 lb. pkg.)

No-chicken bouillon cube (1)Frank's Hot Sauce (.33 cup) No-chicken stock (.66 cup) For Frying: Canola oil (1 cup)Vegenaise

Gluten-free bunsLeaf lettuce Sliced tomato

Directions

Cut the tempeh into three squares and steam over 1 inch of water for about 5-7minutes.

Combine the stock, hot sauce, and bouillon cube in a bowl.

In another dish, sift the onion powder, flour, salt, garlic powder, black pepper,and paprika.

Marinate the steamed tempeh in the hot sauce mixture (15 min.). Warm thecooking oil in a skillet.

Roll the tempeh in the flour mixture and fry until it's golden brown and crispy(10 to 12 min.).

Toast the buns to your liking. Rinse and slice the lettuce and tomatoes.

The tempeh should rest for about two to three minutes before preparing thedelicious sandwiches.

Nutrition: Calories: 510 kcal Fat: 0 g Carbohydrates: 55 g Sodium: 1130 mg

Protein: 29 g

Simple Pizza Recipe

Cooking time: 40 minutesServings: 6-8

Ingredients 1 pizza crust

½ cup tomato sauce

¼ black pepper

1 cup pepperoni slices

1 cup mozzarella cheese1 cup olives

Directions

Place all the toppings on the pizza crust Bake the pizza at 425 F for 12-15 minutes

When ready serve Nutrition: calories 285, fat 10.4g, fiber 3g, protein 5 gThe Boss Burger

Cooking Time: 25 minutes Servings: 3

Ingredients

1-pound ground beef3 cheese slices Worcestershire sauce3 fried eggs

Canned green chilis or verde green sauce (any of your favorite)6 bacon slices, cooked until crisp

Pico de gallo3 burger buns

Pepper & salt to tasteDirections

Heat your grill over high heat.

Season the ground beef with dashes of Worcestershire sauce, pepper & salt.

Make 3 patties from the mixture & cook until you get your desired level ofdoneness.

During the last minute of your cooking time; top each burger with a cheeseslice.

Place on a bun topped with an egg, bacon, a big scoop of pico de gallo & a scoopof verde sauce.

Serve immediately & enjoy.

Nutrition: calories 266 fat 10g Carbohydrates 30g protein 14g fiber 3g

Miso Glazed Salmon

Cooking Time: 10 minutes Servings: 4

Ingredients:

½ cup brown sugar

3 tablespoons soy sauce

¼ cup hot water

3 tablespoons miso (soybean paste)4 salmon fillets

tablespoon butter

tablespoons ginger paste1 tablespoon garlic paste

½ cup sake

1 tablespoon heavy cream

½ cup butter, cut into 8 piecesJuice of half of a lime

For serving:

Steamed snow peas, broccoli, and carrotsSteamed Jasmine Rice

Directions:

Preheat the broiler.

Mix together the brown sugar, soy sauce, hot water, and miso paste. Stir until well combined.

Delicately oil a preparing dish and orchestrate the salmon filets in it. Spoon a few of the miso blend over each filet, clearing out a few for seasoning. Exchangethe dish to the stove and broil for almost 10 minutes. Treat each 3 minutes whereas broiling. In the interim, in a little pan, dissolve 1 tablespoon of butter over medium-high warm.

Add the ginger and garlic paste and cook for about 2 minutes.

Stir in the sake and bring the mixture to a boil. Let it cook for 3 more minutes and add the heavy cream. Cook another 2 minutes, or until the sauce starts to reduce. Then whisk in the remaining butter one piece at a time and cook until thesauce thickens. Expel the pan from the warm and mix within the lime juice.

When the salmon is done, serve by pouring a little sauce over the rice and top with a salmon fillet with vegetables on the side.

Nutrition: Calories: 234 Fat: 34.9 g Carbohydrates: 43 g Protein: 45 g Sodium:

524 mg

Grilled Chicken Tenderloin

Cooking Time: 30 min

Servings: 4 to 5 Ingredients:

4–5 boneless and skinless chicken breasts, cut into strips, or 12 chicken tenderloins, tendons removed

1 cup Italian dressing 2 teaspoons lime juice 4 teaspoons honey Directions:

Combine the dressing, lime juice and honey in a plastic bag. Seal and shake to combine.

Place the chicken in the bag. Seal and shake again, then transfer to the refrigerator for at least 1 hour. The longer it soaked, the more the flavors will imbue into the chicken. When prepared to get ready, exchange the chicken and the marinade to a huge nonstick skillet. Bring to a bubble, at that point diminish the warm and permit stewing until the fluid has cooked down to a coat.

Nutrition: Calories: 451 Fat: 43 g Carbohydrates: 61 g Protein: 65.7 g Sodium:

526 mg

Chicken Parmesan

Cooking Time: 20 minutes Servings 4

Ingredients:

1/2 cup of milk 1 egg

4 chicken breasts, boneless, pounded to 1/2 inches thick Seasoned breadcrumbs

1 (16 Oz) bottle spaghetti sauce Parmesan cheese

Directions:

Whisk together the egg and milk. Dip the breasts of chicken in the mixture of milk and eggs, and then in the crumbs of bread.

Place the chicken in a baking platter.

Put two slices of provolone cheese over each breast.

Pour 1 jar of your favorite spaghetti sauce over everything. Sprinkle with Parmesan cheese and bake for about 25 to 30 minutes at 350 degrees or until bubbly. Serve with marinara Spaghetti.

Nutrition Calories 1290 Total Fat 59grams Total Carbohydrates 116grams Dietary Fiber 11grams Protein 80g

Chicken Piccata

Cooking Time: 15 minutes Servings 4

Ingredients:

4 (4 oz.) chicken breasts 1/4 cup dry White wine 1/2 cup chicken broth

2 tablespoons capers

2 tablespoons Italian parsley, chopped 2 lemons, juiced

2 tablespoons sweet butter1-2 tablespoons olive oil Flour

Salt & pepperDirections:

For Chicken

Season the chicken with salt and pepper. Flour dust in with both hands. Add olive oil in a saucepan and heat over a medium-high flame. Add the chicken to the pan, and sauté until well browned for several minutes. Turn on and cook until browned and cooked thoroughly. Transfer to the platter for moist serving.

For Sauce

Deglaze the sauce with white wine and remove any brown bits that stuck to thepan. Add a broth of chicken, capers, parsley, lemon juice, and butter. Return thechicken to pan and cook, bringing it to a simmer for a short time. Where required, add salt and pepper to taste. Pour over the chicken sauce and serve right away.

Nutrition: Calories 650 Total Fat 24grams Total Carbohydrates 49grams Protein62g

Salmon Oscar

Cooking Time: 15 minutesServings 4

Ingredients:

1/2 lb. of Orzo pasta3 tablespoons butter

1/2 cup Asiago herbal breadcrumbs,1/4 cup soybean oil

1 cup white wine cream sauce,4 tablespoons dried tomatoes 1 cup of asparagus, 1 inch

1/2 lb. sliced. Jumbo lump crab meat4 tablespoons whole butter

1/2 lemon, juiced

1 tablespoon basil, chopped

1 tablespoon parsley, choppedAsiago Herb Breadcrumbs:

1 cup Asiago cheese, rubbed1 cup fresh breadcrumbs

1 tablespoon basil, chopped

1 tablespoon parsley, choppedWhite Wine Cream Sauce:

1 tablespoon butter

tablespoon garlic, chopped1/4 cup dry white wine

Directions:

To make Pasta

Cook orzo pasta to al dente 2 minutes short of packaging directions To prepare the Sauce

Sauté the garlic and butter in a small saucepan until the garlic is softened.

Add the white wine into the pan and bring it to a simmer; until half the wine is left. Add heavy cream and chicken broth; let it boil for 5-7 minutes or until the sauce starts to thicken. Turn the heat off and set aside.

Heat 3 tablespoons butter in another sauté pan and cook Orzo for about 2 minutes, finish with grated parmesan cheese, and put it in the center of a large serving platter.

To make Salmon

Mixed the salmon with salt and pepper, at that point press the salmon confront side into the breadcrumbs of the asiago herb until fully coated on one side. Cook the salmon (breaded side down) for around 3 or 4 minutes or until golden brown. Place the salmon atop the Orzo. Place the white wine cream sauce with the sun-dried tomatoes, jumbo lump crab meat, asparagus, whole butter and 1/2 lemon juice into an 8 "sauté pan and bring to a simmer; cook for 30 seconds. Place the ingredients on top and around the salmon and pour the sauce around the salmon and Orzo. Decorate with lemon wedges.

Nutrition: Calories 1160 Total Fat 86grams Total Carbohydrates 24grams Protein 77g

Beef Tenderloin Medallions

Cooking Time: 25 minutes Servings 4

Ingredients:

1-ounce mixed dried wild mushrooms2 cups of beef broth

teaspoons of canola oil,

1 tablespoon butter, softened

1/4 cup shallot

1 teaspoon roasted garlic

3 cup dry white wine

3 cup whipping cream

8 (4 Oz) beef medal.

1/4 teaspoon salt

1/4 teaspoon pepperDirections:

Preheat oven to 350 ° C.

Sauce: Place the mushrooms in a warm broth bowl and soak them for 20 minutesor until tender. Strain mushrooms and keep the broth in stock. Add 1 tablespoonof oil, butter, shallots, garlic paste, and mushrooms to a large saucepan on medium-high heat. Cook for about 5 minutes, until shallots are caramelized. Addwine and deglaze the pan, about three minutes. Add the broth and boil next, allowing the liquid to shrink by half, around 5-8 minutes. Add milk, then cook for another 2 minutes.

Beef: Season the beef with salt and pepper in the meantime. Add remaining oil on high heat to an ovenproof skillet and pan-sear beef and put in the oven for 1minute per side. Cook for around 7-19 minutes or until medium hits 160 degreesfor an instant-read thermometer. Take the beef off the stove and set aside to rest.

Nutrition: Calories 910 Total Fat 57grams Total Carbohydrates 47grams Protein

59g

Red Lobster's Garlic Shrimp Scampi

Preparation Time: 15 minutesCooking Time: 15 minutes Servings: 4

Ingredients

1-pound shrimp, peeled and deveinedSalt and pepper to taste

1 tablespoon olive oil

3 garlic cloves, finely chopped 1 ½ white wine

2 tablespoons lemon juice

¼ teaspoon dried basil

¼ teaspoon dried oregano

¼ teaspoon dried rosemary

¼ teaspoon dried thyme

½ cup butter

2 tablespoons parsley leaves, minced

¼ cup Parmesan cheese, shredded (optional)

Directions

Flavor shrimp with salt and pepper.

In a pan with heated oil, sauté shrimp on medium-high heat for about 2 minutesor until color changes to pink. Transfer onto a plate for later.

In the same pan, sauté garlic for 30 seconds or until aromatic. Pour in white wineand lemon juice. Stir, then bring to a boil. Adjust heat to medium-low and cookfor an additional 4 minutes. Mix in basil, oregano, rosemary, and thyme. Then, add butter gradually. Mix until completely melted and blended with otheringredients. Remove from heat.

Return shrimp to pan and add parsley. Taste and adjust seasoning with salt and pepper as needed.

Sprinkle Parmesan on top, if desired. Serve.

Nutrition: Calories 448, Total Fat 29 g, Carbohydrates 3 g, Protein 26 g, Sodium362 mg

Bonefish Grill's Bang Shrimp

Preparation Time: 5 minutesCooking Time: 5 minutes Servings: 4

Ingredients

½ cup mayonnaise

¼ cup Thai sweet chili sauce

3-5 drops hot chili sauce (or more if you like it spicier)

½ cup cornstarch

1-pound small shrimp, peeled and deveined1 ½ cups vegetable oil

Directions

To make the sauce, combine mayonnaise with Thai chili sauce and hot chilisauce in a bowl.

In a separate bowl, add cornstarch. Toss shrimp in cornstarch until well-coated.

Heat oil in a wok. Fry shrimp until golden brown, about 2-3 minutes. Transferonto a plate lined with paper towels to drain excess oil.

Serve shrimp in a bowl with sauce drizzled on top.

Nutrition: Calories 274, Total Fat 11 g, Carbohydrates 26 g, Protein 16 g,

Sodium 1086 mg

Chi-Chi's Seafood Chimichanga

Cooking Time: 30 minutes Servings: 6

Ingredients

4 tablespoons butter

4 tablespoons flour

½ teaspoon butter

2 dashes black pepper, ground2 cups milk

8 ounces jack cheese, shredded

1 16-ounce package crab meat, flaked1 cup cottage cheese

¼ cup Parmesan cheese1 egg

1 tablespoon dried parsley flakes

¼ teaspoon onion powder1 tablespoon lemon juice

Shredded lettuce for serving

¼ cup sliced green onions for garnishDirections:

Preheat oven to 375°F.

To make the sauce, heat butter in a pan on medium heat. Add flour, salt, and pepper. Mix, then pour in milk. Stirring often, cook until sauce is thick then simmer for an additional 1 minute.

Turn off heat and stir in jack cheese until completely blended into sauce.

In a bowl, combine crab meat, cottage and Parmesan cheese, egg, parsley, and onion powder.

Heat tortillas in microwave for 10 seconds or until warm. Wet bottom side of tortilla and add crab meat mixture on top. Fold tortilla to wrap filling.

Coat baking sheet with cooking spray. Bake chimichangas for about 25 minutes.Reheat sauce until warm. Mix in lemon juice and stir until blended.

Transfer chimichangas to plates over a bed of shredded lettuce, if desired. Topwith sauce and garnish with green onions before serving.

Nutrition: Calories 794, Total Fat 33 g, Carbohydrates 77 g, Protein 44 g,

Sodium 1932 mg

Red Lobster's Lobster Pizza

Cooking Time: 5 minutes Servings: 1

Ingredients

10-inch flour tortillas

1-ounce roasted garlic butter

tablespoons Parmesan cheese, shredded

1/2 cup fresh Roma tomatoes, finely chopped2 tablespoons fresh basil, cut into thin strips2 ounces lobster meat, chopped

½ cup Italian cheese blend, gratedVegetable oil for coating

Dash salt and pepper

Fresh lemon juice for servingDirections:

Preheat oven to 450°F.

Coat one side of tortilla with garlic butter. Top with Parmesan cheese, tomatoes,basil, lobster meat, and Italian cheese blend in that order. Set aside.

Prepare a pizza pan. Apply a light coat of vegetable oil and cover with a sprint ofsalt and pepper. Exchange pizza onto container. Prepare for around 5 minutes. Cut into cuts and sprinkle with lemon juice. Once you are accustomed to eatinghealthy and nutritious food at home, you may find that you are looking elsewhere.

Cut into slices and drizzle with lemon juice.Serve.

Nutrition: Calories 339, Total Fat 10 g, Carbohydrates 41 g, Protein 22 g, Sodium 890 mg

Pesto Cavatappi from Noodles & Company

Preparation Time: 5 minutes**Cooking Time**: 20 minutesServing: 8

Ingredients

4 quarts water

1 tablespoon salt

1-pound macaroni pasta1 teaspoon olive oil

1 large tomato, finely chopped

4-ounce mushrooms, finely chopped

¼ cup chicken broth

¼ cup dry white wine

¼ cup heavy cream1 cup pesto

cup Parmesan cheese, grated Directions

Add water and salt to a pot. Bring to a boil. Put in pasta and cook for 10 minutesor until al dente. Drain and set aside.

In a pan, heat oil. Sauté tomatoes and mushrooms for 5 minutes. Pour in broth, wine, and cream. Bring to a boil. Reduce heat to medium and simmer for 2 minutes or until mixture is thick. Stir in pesto and cook for another 2 minutes. Toss in pasta. Mix until fully coated.

Transfer onto plates and sprinkle with Parmesan cheese.

Nutrition: Calories 655, Total Fat 38 g, Carbs 47 g, Protein 31 g, Sodium 359 mg

Cajun Chicken Pasta from Chili's

Preparation Time: 10 minutes**Cooking** Time: 20 minutes Servings: 4

Ingredients

chicken breasts, boneless and skinless 1 tablespoon olive oil, divided

1 tablespoon Cajun seasoning 3 quarts water

½ tablespoon salt

8 ounces penne pasta

2 tablespoons unsalted butter 3 garlic cloves, minced

1 cup heavy cream

½ teaspoon lemon zest

¼ cup Parmesan cheese, shredded Salt and black pepper, to taste

tablespoon oil

Roma tomatoes, diced

2 tablespoons parsley chopped Directions

Place chicken in a Ziploc bag. Add 1 tablespoon oil and Cajun seasoning. Usingyour hands, combine chicken and mixture until well-coated. Seal tightly and setaside to marinate.

Cook pasta in a pot filled with salt and boiling water. Follow package instructions. Drain and set aside.

In a skillet, heat butter over medium heat. Sauté garlic for 1 minute or until aromatic. Slowly add cream, followed by lemon zest. Cook for 1 minute, stirringcontinuously until fully blended. Toss in Parmesan cheese. Mix until sauce is alittle thick, then add salt and pepper. Add pasta and combine until well-coated. Transfer onto a bowl and keep warm.

In a separate skillet, heat remaining oil. Transfer onto chopping board and cut into thin strips.

Top pasta with chicken and sprinkle with tomatoes and parsley on top.Serve.

Nutrition: Calories 625, Total Fat 28 g, Carbs 27 g, Protein 31 g, Sodium 339mg

Chow Mein from Panda Express

Cooking Time: 10 minutes Servings 4

Ingredients

8 quarts water

12 ounces Yakisoba noodles

¼ cup soy sauce

2 teaspoons ginger, grated

¼ teaspoon white pepper, ground2 tablespoons olive oil

1 onion, finely chopped

celery stalks, sliced on the bias2 cups cabbage, chopped Directions

In a pot, bring water to a boil. Cook Yakisoba noodles for about 1 minute untilnoodles separate. Drain and set aside.

Combine soy sauce, garlic, brown sugar, ginger, and white pepper in a bowl.

In a pan, heat oil on medium-high heat. Sauté onion and celery for 3 minutes oruntil soft. Add cabbage and stir-fry for an additional minute. Mix in noodles andsoy sauce mixture. Cook for 2 minutes, stirring continuously until noodles are well-coated.

Transfer into bowls. Serve.

Nutrition: Calories 382, Total Fat 8 g, Carbs 72 g, Protein 14 g, Sodium 1194 mg

Rattlesnake Pasta from Pizzeria Uno

Preparation Time: 5 minutes**Cooking Time**: 25 minutesServings: 6

IngredientsPasta:

quarts

1-pound penne pasta1 dash of salt Chicken:

2 tablespoons butter

2 cloves garlic, finely chopped

½ tablespoon Italian seasoning

1-pound chicken breast, boneless and skinless, cut into small squaresSauce:

4 tablespoons butter

2 cloves garlic, finely chopped

¼ cup all-purpose flour1 tablespoon salt

¾ teaspoon white pepper2 cups milk

cup half-and-half

¾ cup Parmesan cheese, shredded8 ounces Colby cheese, shredded3 jalapeno peppers, chopped Directions

In a pot of boiling water, add salt, and cook pasta according to packageinstructions. Drain well and set aside.

To prepare the chicken, heat butter in a pan. Sauté garlic and Italian seasoning for 1 minute. Add chicken and cook 5-7 minutes or until cooked thoroughly, flipping half way through. Transfer onto a plate once. Set aside.

In the same pan, prepare the sauce. Add butter and heat until melted. Stir in garlic and cook for 30 seconds. Then, add flour, salt, and pepper. Cook for 2 more minutes, stirring continuously. Pour in milk and half-and-half. Keepstirring until sauce turns thick and smooth.

Toss in chicken, jalapeno peppers, and pasta. Stir until combined.Serve.

Nutrition: Calories 835, Total Fat 44 g, Carbs 72 g, Protein 40 g, Sodium 1791mg

Copycat Kung Pao Spaghetti from California Pizza

Kitchen

Preparation Time: 10 minutesCooking Time: 20 minutes Servings: 4

Ingredients

1-pound spaghetti

tablespoons vegetable oil

chicken breasts, boneless and skinlessSalt and pepper, to taste

garlic cloves, finely chopped

½ cup dry roasted peanuts

6 green onions, cut into half-inch pieces10-12 Dried bird eyes hot peppers Sauce:

½ cup soy sauce

½ cup chicken broth

½ cup dry sherry

2 tablespoons red chili paste with garlic

¼ cup sugar

2 tablespoons red wine vinegar2 tablespoons cornstarch

tablespoon sesame oilDirections

Follow instructions on package to cook spaghetti noodles. Drain and set aside.

Add oil to a large pan over medium-high heat. Generously season chicken withsalt and pepper, then add to pan once hot. Cook for about 3 to 4 minutes. Turn chicken over and cook for another 3 to 4 minutes. Remove from heat and allowto cool.

Once chicken is cool enough to handle, chop chicken into small pieces. Set aside.

Return pan to heat. Add garlic and sauté for about 1 minute until aromatic. Pourin prepared sauce, then stir. Add pasta, cooked chicken, peanuts, hot peppers, and scallions. Mix well.

Serve.

Nutrition: calories 548, total fat 22 g, saturated fat 7 g,

carbs 67 g, sugar 16 g, fibers 4 g, protein 15 g, sodium 2028 mg

Three Cheese Chicken Penne from Applebee's

Cooking Time: 1 hour Servings: 4

Ingredients

boneless chicken

1 cup Italian salad dressing

cups penne pasta

6 tablespoons olive oil, divided15 ounces Alfredo sauce

8 ounces combination mozzarella, Parmesan, and provolone cheeses, grated4 roma tomatoes, seeded and diced

4 tablespoons fresh basil, diced2 cloves garlic, finely chopped

Shredded parmesan cheese for servingDirections

Preheat oven to 350°F.

In a bowl, add chicken then drizzle with Italian dressing. Mix to fully coat chicken with dressing. Cover using plastic wrap and keep inside refrigerator overnight but, if you're in a hurry, at least 2 hours is fine.

Follow instructions on package to cook penne pasta. Drain, then set aside.

Brush 3 tablespoons oil onto grates of grill then preheat to medium-high heat. Add marinated chicken onto grill, discarding the marinade. Cook chicken until both sides are fully cooked and internal temperature measures 165°F. Remove from grill. Set aside until cool enough to handle. Then, cut chicken into thin slices.

In a large bowl, add cooked noodles, Alfredo sauce, and grilled chicken. Mix until combined.

Drizzle remaining oil onto large casserole pan, then pour noodle mixture inside.Sprinkle cheeses on top. Remove from oven.

Mix tomatoes, basil, and garlic in a bowl. Add on top of pasta.Sprinkle parmesan cheese before serving.

Nutrition: 1402, total fat 93 g, saturated fat 27 g, carbs 91 g, sugar 7 g, fibers 3g, protein 62 g, sodium 5706 mg

Boston Market Mac n' Cheese

Cooking Time: 20 minutes Servings: 6

Ingredients

8-ounce package spiral pasta2 tablespoons butter

tablespoons all-purpose flour1 ¾ cups whole milk

¼ cups diced processed cheese like Velveeta™

¼ teaspoon dry mustard

½ teaspoon onion powder1 teaspoon salt

Pepper, to tasteDirections

Cook pasta according to package instructions. Drain, then set aside.

To prepare sauce make the roux with four and butter over medium-low heat in alarge deep skillet. Add milk and whisk until well blended.

Add cheese, mustard,

salt, and pepper. Keep stirring until smooth.

Once pasta is cooked, transfer to a serving bowl. Pour cheese mixture on top. Toss to combine.

Serve warm.

Nutrition: calories 319, total fat 17 g, saturated fat 10 g,

carbs 28 g, sugar 7 g, fibers 1 g, protein 17 g, sodium 1134 mg

Macaroni Grill's Pasta Milano

Preparation Time: 5 minutesCooking Time: 20 minutes Servings: 6

Ingredients

1-pound bowtie pasta2 teaspoons olive oil

1-pound chicken, chopped into small pieces1 12-ounce package mushrooms, chopped 1 cup onion, minced

garlic cloves, finely minced

½ cup sun dried tomatoes, diced1 ½ cups half and half

1 tablespoon butter, softened

½ cup Parmesan cheese, shredded, plus some more for serving1 teaspoon black pepper, ground

1 tablespoon fresh basil, mincedDirections

Follow instructions on package to cook bowtie pasta. Drain, then set aside.

Add oil to a pan over medium-high heat. Once hot, add chicken and stir-fry forabout 5 to 6 minutes until cooked through. Set chicken aside onto a plate.

In the same pan, toss in mushrooms, onions, garlic, and sun-dried tomatoes. Sauté until onions turn soft and mushrooms become a light brown, then sprinklesalt and pepper to season. Return chicken to pan and mix.

Mix half and half, butter, Parmesan, pepper, and basil in a small bowl.

Add half and half mixture to pan. Stir, and let simmer for about 3 to 4 minutes oruntil pan ingredients are thoroughly heated. Mix in pasta until coated well.

Serve.

Nutrition: calories 600, total fat 18 g, saturated fat 9 g, carbs 69 g, sugar 8 g,fibers 5 g, protein 42 g, sodium 349 mg

Papa John's Cinnapie

Preparation Time: 5 min**Cooking Time**: 12 min
Servings: 12

Ingredients

1 whole pizza dough

tablespoon melted butter

tablespoons cinnamon, or to tasteTopping

¾ cup flour

½ cup white sugar

⅓ cup brown sugar2 tablespoons oil

2 tablespoons shorteningIcing

1½ cups powdered sugar3 tablespoons milk

¾ teaspoon vanilla

Directions

Preheat oven to 460°F. Grease or spray a pizza pan or baking sheet.Brush the dough evenly with melted butter.

Sprinkle with cinnamon.

Place the ingredients for the topping in a bowl and toss together with a fork.Sprinkle topping over dough.

Bake until fragrant and lightly browned at the edges (about 10–12 minutes).

Mix the icing ingredients together in a bowl. If too thick, gradually add in a littlemore milk.

Drizzle icing over warm pizza.

Nutrition: Calories 560, Total Fat 19 g, Carbs 90 g, Protein 1 g, Sodium 540 mg

Cici's Apple Pizza

Preparation time: 40 minCooking time: 20–30 min
Servings: 8

IngredientsCrust

2 tablespoons sugar

1 tablespoon yeast

1½ cups warm water, about 105–110°F4
tablespoons butter, softened

3 cups bread flour

½ teaspoon saltApple Topping

4 tablespoons butter, softened

⅔ cup brown sugar

⅔ cup bread flour

1 teaspoon cinnamonGlaze

1 tablespoon milk

teaspoon butter

cups powdered sugarDirections

Prepare the crust. Preheat oven to 350°F. In a mixer bowl, dissolve sugar and yeast in warm water. Add softened butter. Add the flour and salt. Using the dough hook, knead to make a smooth, sticky dough (about 5 minutes).

Prepare the topping. Chop the apple pieces.

Spread apple pie filling over baked crust and sprinkle evenly with crumbtopping.

Bake until fragrant and lightly browned at the edges (about 10–15 minutes).

Prepare the glaze while the pie is baking. Place ingredients in a saucepan over low heat, stirring continuously until smooth. Add a few drops of water or milk if too thick.

Cool the pizza slightly (about 5 minutes) and then drizzle with glaze.Let stand while glaze sets (about 5 minutes) and then serve.

Nutrition: Calories 149, Total Fat 3.6 g,Carbs 26.2 g, Protein 3 g, Sodium 0 mg

Taco Bell's Caramel Empanadas

Preparation time: 20 min Cooking time: 4–10 min
Servings: 4

Ingredients

1 tablespoon flour

¼ cup sugar

1 teaspoon cinnamon

4 medium apples, peeled, cored and diced

¼ cup water (optional).

¼ cup caramel sauce2 tablespoons butter

2 premade pie crusts (dough)1 egg white

Oil, for frying (optional)Cinnamon Sugar Coating

¼ cup granulated sugar1½ teaspoons cinnamon

Directions

Preheat oven to 400°F and line a baking sheet with parchment paper.Mix flour, sugar and cinnamon together in a bowl. Set aside.

Place diced apples and water in a saucepan and bring to a boil. Reduce to a simmer and cook until apples are tender. Remove from heat. (If you prefer crispapple in the filling, skip this step and eliminate water from recipe.)

Mix flour mixture into apples.

Add caramel sauce and butter. Set aside.

Take premade dough out of the refrigerator about 15 minutes before use. Roll out to about 10 inches in diameter. Use a bowl (about 5 inches in diameter) to cut out circles in the dough. Use a smaller bowl to make mini-empanadas.

Spoon filling into the center of each dough circle. Brush egg white along the edges.

Fold the dough over like a turnover.

Press down on the edges using a fork, to seal.Brush with egg white.

Combine ingredients for cinnamon sugar.

Sprinkle empanadas with cinnamon sugar and bake until golden brown (about 15minutes).

The empanadas may also be deep fried (about 2–3 minutes on each side). Drainon paper towels and sprinkle cinnamon sugar *after* frying.

Nutrition: Calories 149, Total Fat 3.6 g, Carbs 26.2 g, Protein 3 g, Sodium 0 mg

Pizza Hut's Cherry Pizza

Preparation time: 40 minCooking time: 20–30 min Servings: 8

IngredientsCrust

2 tablespoons sugar

1 tablespoon yeast 1½ cups warm water

4 tablespoons butter, softened3 cups flour

½ teaspoon salt

Cherry Topping and Streusel

1 (20-ounce) can cherry pie filling4 tablespoons butter, softened

⅔ cup brown sugar

⅔ cup bread flour

1 teaspoon cinnamonGlaze

1 tablespoon milk

teaspoon of butter

cups powdered sugarDirections

Prepare the crust. Preheat oven to 350°F. In a mixer bowl, dissolve sugar and yeast in warm water. Add softened butter. Add the flour and salt. Using the dough hook, knead to make a smooth, sticky dough (about 5 minutes). Bake for 15 minutes.

Prepare the topping. Empty the can of cherry filling into a bowl and set aside. Tomake the streusel, combine the butter, brown sugar, bread flour and cinnamon ina separate bowl.

Spread cherry pie filling over baked crust and sprinkle evenly with the streusel.Bake until fragrant and lightly browned at the edges (about 10–15 minutes).

Prepare the glaze while the pie is baking. Place ingredients in a saucepan over low heat, stirring continuously until smooth

.Let stand to set glaze (about 5 minutes) and serve.

Nutrition: Calories 186, Total Fat 53 g, Carbs 32 g, Protein 1 g, Sodium 90 mg

Ruby Tuesday's Apple Pie

Preparation time: 15 min plus 30 min thawing
Cooking time: 60–70 min

Servings: 8Ingredients

1 (9-inch) frozen apple pie

½ cup (1 stick) butter

1 cup brown sugar, packed, divided3½ teaspoons cinnamon, divided

¼ teaspoon allspice

¼ teaspoon cloves

1½ teaspoons lemon juice

¾ cup flour

½ cup sugar

10 tablespoons frozen butter

1 cup chopped walnuts (optional)

½ gallon vanilla ice creamDirection

Allow pie to thaw as you prepare the other ingredients (about 30–45 minutes). Make a temporary hole in the pie by cutting an X in the center.

Preheat oven to 350°F.

Whisk in ½ cup brown sugar, 1½ teaspoons cinnamon, the allspice, cloves and lemon juice. As soon as sugar is fully dissolved, remove from heat.

Carefully open up the X in the pie by folding back the crust. Pour the butter mixture through the hole, slanting the pie from side to side to distribute the filling. Reseal the X and make a few small vent holes in the crust.

Bake for 30 minutes and remove from oven. Turn oven temperature down to 325°F.

Set up the garnish. Mesh the frozen spread and throw with flour, remainingsugars, remaining cinnamon, and pecans, whenever wanted.

Sprinkle beating over pie.

Heat until filling is foaming and hull is brilliant earthy colored (around 30–40 minutes). Eliminate from broiler and let cool for 10–15 minutes.

Cut into wedges and present with scoops of vanilla *frozen yogurt.*

Nourishment: Calories 493, Total Fat 34 g, Carbs 46 g, Protein 4 g, Sodium 174 mg

Tommy Bahama's Key Lime Pie

Planning time: 40 minCooking time: 50 min
Servings: 2

FixingsPie:

10-inch graham ~~shrustthyel~~ egg white

2½ cups improved dense milk

¾ cup purified egg yolk 1 cup lime juice

1 lime, zing

1 lime, cut into 8

White Chocolate Mousse Whipped Cream:8 liquid ounces weighty cream

3 tablespoons powdered sugar

¼ teaspoon unadulterated vanilla concentrate

½ tablespoon white chocolate mousse moment blend

Headings

Preheat the broiler to 350°F while brushing the graham saltine outside layer with the eggwhite. Cover the outside layer totally prior to setting it in the broiler to heat for 5 minutes.

Whip the egg yolk and dense milk together until they are mixed totally. Add the lime squeeze and zing to the combination and keep whipping until the blend is smooth.

   At the point when the outside has cooled, include the egg combination and prepare at 250°F for 25 to 30 minutes.

At the point when the pie is cooked, place it on a cooling rack to cool. At that point place it in the fridge for in any event two hours.

While trusting that the pie will cool, beat the initial three whipped cream elements for two minutes (if utilizing a hand blender). At the point when the blend is smooth, include the chocolate mousse and beat to solid pinnacles.

Eliminate the pie from the cooler, cut it into eight pieces, and embellishment each with the white chocolate mousse whipped cream and a cut of lime. Serve.

Nourishment: Calories 500, Total Fat 9g, Carbs 26 g, Protein 1 g, Sodium 110 mg

TCBY's Chocolate Yogurt Pie

Preparation time: 10 minCooking time: 8 h 30 min

Servings: 2Ingredients

⅔ cup butter 1¼ cups sugar

1 cup unsweetened cocoa powder

¼ teaspoon salt

½ teaspoon vanilla extract2 large eggs

½ cup all-purpose flour

1-pint TCBY chocolate yogurtWhipped cream

Caramel syrup

Directions

Before you begin, preheat the oven to 325°F.

Place a heatproof bowl in simmering water and mix the butter, sugar, cocoa powder and salt over the heat.

Continue stirring and heating the mixture until it becomes smooth. Remove the bowl from the heat and set aside.

When the mixture becomes a little cooler, mix in the vanilla extract and the eggs, one at a time. Make sure that the mixture is not too hot so that the eggs do not get cooked.

Beat the flour into the mixture with a wooden spoon until the entire mixture is thoroughly blended.

Transfer the mixture to a greased baking pan and then bake for 20 to 25 minutes. Remove the pie from the oven and transfer to a cooling rack.

When the pie has cooled down, spread frozen yogurt over the surface and freeze for 10 to 15 minutes.

Garnish the yogurt pie with whipped cream and caramel syrup, and then return to the freezer for at least 8 hours.

Cut the pie into equal portions and serve.

Nutrition: Calories 330, Total Fat 13 g, Carbs 49 g, Protein 4 g, Sodium 160 mg

Macaroni Grill Focaccia

Preparation time: 1hr 10mins|Cooking time: 30 mins Servings: 6-8

Ingredients:

9 tablespoons olive oil (divided use)3/4 cup of unshifted semolina flour

1 1/2 Tbsp. of fast-rising active dry yeast3 cups of unshifted all-purpose flour

1/2 teaspoon of salt (shared)

1 1/2 cups of warm milk (between 120 and 130 degrees)1 tablespoon of fresh rosemary leaves.

Directions

Pour a small tablespoon of olive oil into a cake pan of 9 "square; spread evenlyto cover the bottom and sides. Add all-purpose flour, semolina flour, 2 tablespoons of olive oil, 1/4 teaspoon of salt, and all the yeast in the bowl of a mixer fitted with a dough hook (mixing can be done by hand).

Mix ingredients over medium velocity. Reduce the speed to low and add milk gradually. Boost the speed to medium, and proceed to mix for 5 minutes (kneadby hand for around 8 to 10 minutes) Sprinkle with a little flour at the bottom ofthe cake pan. Remove the dough from the bowl and uniformly spread out in thepan. Cover with a towel and take 30 minutes of rest.

Preheat oven to 400 degrees F. Towel cover. Clean the dough with 1 to 2 olive oil tablespoons.

Sprinkle with extra salt and rosemary over the top. Bake for another 20 minutes. Drizzle with remaining oil and remove from the oven.

Nutrition: Calories from Fat 211 g, Total Fat 23.5 g, Saturated Fat 4.3 g, Cholesterol 8.5 mg, Sodium 227.1 mg, Total Carbohydrate 66.9 g, Dietary Fiber

3.2 g, Sugars 0g, Protein 12.3 g

Grilled Eggplant Cheese Less Pizza

Preparation time: 1hr 10mins|Cooking time: 30 mins Servings: 6-8

Ingredients:

3 tablespoons olive oil1/2 teaspoon soy sauce

prepared pizza dough, as needed1/4 teaspoon cumin

a pinch of cayenne pepper4 thick Japanese eggplants 1 red onion

2 tablespoons of fresh coriander,

4 cups of fresh spinach chopped, 1/4 cut in Strips6 tomato

es, julienned

extra virgin olive oil Balsamic vinegar (optional). Directions:

Rinse eggplants and dry them—place on a cutting board, and slice in about 1/8-inch slices lengthwise. Dispose of unused eggplant, and set aside the slices. Slicethe red onion into 1/8 "thick rings instead. Set out around 2/3 cup of onion ringsin a measuring cup, remove any remaining.

Preheat an outdoor barbeque or indoor barbecue. In a small cup, blend 1tablespoon of olive oil with soy sauce, cumin, and cayenne and mix to match. Use a brush or other utensil, powder mixture gently on both sides of eggplant slices. Place on grill and grill for about 2-3 minutes. Switch off the grill, then remove it from the grill and set aside.

Preheat the oven to 500 ° C. Shape the dough into two 9-inch rounds using prepared pizza dough. Wash each one with 1 spoonful of olive oil. The onion rings are then scattered over the two rounds of pizza. Brush over onion with grilled eggplant.

Place the two pizzas on a sheet of cookies and put them into the preheated oven.Bake at 500 for about 8 minutes until crusts are golden. Take off the oven and allow to cool partially.

Slice pizzas, then top with the spinach and cilantro. Sprinkle with chopped tomato. Serve alongside with oil and vinegar, if needed.

Nutrition: 1340Calories, Total Fat 90g, Saturated Fat 16g, Trans Fat 0.5g, Cholesterol 220mg, Sodium 1520mg, Total Carbohydrate 103g, Dietary Fiber 10g, Sugars 15g, Protein 34g

Penne Rustica

Preparation time: 30 minutesCooking time: 30 mins Servings: 10

Ingredients:

Gratinate Sauce 4 1/2 Cups2 teaspoons butter

2 teaspoons chopped garlic1 teaspoon Dijon mustard

1 teaspoon chopped rosemary1 teaspoon dill

1 cup marsala wine

1/4 teaspoon cayenne pepper8 cups heavy cream

Penne Rustic:

1-ounce pancetta or 1-ounce bacon18 shrimp, peeled and deveined

12 ounces grilled chicken breasts, sliced16 -24 ounces penne pasta, cooked

3 teaspoons chopped pimiento6 ounces butter

1 teaspoon chopped shallot1 pinch salt and pepper

1 cup parmesan cheese1/2 teaspoon paprika

6 sprigs fresh rosemaryDirections:

For Gratinata Sauce:

Saute butter, garlic, and rosemary before browning starts.Add Marsala wine, and diminish by one third.

Add remaining ingredients and raising the original volume by half.Rest aside.

Saute pancetta until it begins to brown for Penne Rustica.Add butter, shallots, and shrimp to taste.

Cook until the shrimp is uniformly white and translucent.Stir in rice, salt, pepper, and blend well.

Add 1/2 cup parmesan cheese and gratinata sauce. Simmer until sauce becomes thick.

Combine the shrimp & chicken mixture in a large bowl with the cooked pasta.Pour into a large saucepan or roaster dish.

Top with the remaining cheese, sprinkle with the pimientos, and paprika. Bakefor 10 to 15 minutes, at 475 degrees.

Use fresh rosemary sprig to garnish.

Nutrition: Carbs 82g, Dietary Fiber 3g, Sugar 5g, Fat 52g, Saturated 21g, Trans1g, Protein 66g

Lobster Ravioli

Preparation time: 1hourCooking time: 30 mins Servings: 8 Ingredients:

Substitute lobster meat for the shrimp. Ravioli De Gamberi Grill Macaroni Pasta1 lb. Flour

4 Eggs

1 Tbsp. Olive oil1 Tbsp. Water

1 Tsp Salt Directions:

Put the flour over a clean, dry surface in a mound. Form a well or a hole in the flour center. Break the eggs into the flour center and add the butter, water, and salt. Mix the ingredients using your hands and gradually pour in the flour. Kneaduntil it has blended well. Cover with a clean wet cloth and let it rest for 30 minutes to rest. Break the butter into pieces. Start passing the dough through a pasta machine and continue running through it until it's smooth. Run the doughin the thinnest setting to shape four sheets of dough.

Nutrition: 1240Calories, Total Fat 70g, Saturated Fat 15g, Trans Fat 0.5g, Cholesterol 120mg, Sodium 1320mg, Total Carbohydrate 103g, Dietary Fiber 10g, Sugars 15g, Protein 34g

Stuffing Shrimp

Preparation time: 1hr 10mins|Cooking time: 30 mins Servings: 6-8

Ingredients

1 Tbsp. Butter

1 Tbsp. Olive oil

1 1/2 lbs. of shrimp cleaned and deveined2 leeks, white part, chopped

1/2 tsp salt

1/4 tsp Ground Pepper White1 lb. ricotta cheese

1 Egg

1/4 C Heavy Cream

Tbsp. Fresh Basil, finely chopped 1/2 Tbsp. Fresh thyme, finely choppedDirections:

Add olive oil and butter in a saucepot. Add shrimps, leeks, salt, and pepper to taste. Cook for four minutes. Remove 1/2 shrimp, then set aside. Combine the ricotta cheese, milk, butter, basil, and thyme in a bowl and blend. Combine the mixture of cooled shrimps and the leek.

Nutrition: 720Calories, Total Fat 74g, Saturated Fat 46g, Trans Fat 3g, Cholesterol 340mg, Sodium 1390mg, Total Carbohydrate 36g, Dietary Fiber 3g,Sugars 3g, Protein 31g

Lemon Butter Sauce:

Preparation time: 40 minutesCooking time: 30 mins Servings: 6-8

Ingredients

1⁄2 Cups Sauce.

1/4 Cups dry White wine. 1⁄2 Tbsp. of minced garlic

1⁄2 tsp of Saffron-replace with 1/4 tsp turmeric. 1⁄2 tsp white ground pepper

juice from lemon

1 Cup Heavy Cream 1⁄2 lb. cooked shrimp Directions:

Melt butter in a sauté pan. Add the garlic, saffron, and pepper to taste. Sauté onfor two minutes. Add white wine and proceed to cook for 1 minute. Add milk and lemon juice. Cook well until mixed. Add shrimp cooked, and cook for 1 minute.

Serve the ravioli in a bowl of boiling salted water for around 2 -3 minutes. Remove and extract from the water. Place ravioli in a pot, and sauce over.

Nutrition: 920Calories, Total Fat 74g, Saturated Fat 46g, Trans Fat 3g, Cholesterol 340mg, Sodium 1390mg, Total Carbohydrate 36g, Dietary Fiber 3g,Sugars 3g, Protein 31g

Chili: Wendy's Copycat

Preparation Time: 1 hour 10 minutes

Cooking Time: 25

Servings: 6Ingredients:

Olive oil (2 tbsp.)Medium onion (1)

Celery (2 stalks)

Medium green bell pepper (1)Tomato paste (1 tbsp.) Ground beef (1.5 lb.)

Chili powder (3 tbsp.)Ground cumin (2 tsp.)Garlic powder (1 tsp.)

Black pepper & kosher salt (as desired)Crushed tomatoes (28-oz. can)

Kidney & Pinto beans (15-oz. can of each)Note: Reserve the juices in the beans.

For Serving:

Shredded cheddar Sliced green onionsDirection:

Use the medium temperature setting to warm a skillet with the oil. Mince/chop and sauté the onions, celery, and bell peppers (5 min.).

Stir in the tomato paste and stir (2 min.) and add the beef to simmer another six minutes. Drain the fat and place the meat back on the burner. Add in the chili powder, pepper, salt, garlic powder, and cumin.

Pour in the tomatoes, plus a half of a can of water to remove the remainder of thejuices. Add the beans and liquids.

Stir well and wait for it to boil. Once boiling, set the temperature on low andsimmer for an additional 40 minutes.

Adjust seasonings as desired and serve with fresh onions and cheddar as desired.

Nutrition: Calories: 63 Fat: 40 g Saturated Fat: 16 g Carbs: 39 g, Fibers: 3 g

Protein: 28 g Sodium: 1281 mg

Clam-Potato Chowder: Red Lobster Copycat

Preparation Time: 45 minutesCooking Time: 25

Servings: 6Ingredients:

Minced clams (2 each - 6.5 oz. cans)Crispy bacon (2 strips)

Medium onion (1)

All-purpose flour (2 tbsp.) Potatoes (4 medium/1.75 lb.)Water (1 cup)

Dried savory (.25 tsp.)Salt (.5 tsp.)

Black pepper (pinch) Dried thyme (.25-.5 tsp.)2% milk (2 cups)

Freshly minced parsley (2 tbsp.)Direction:

Drain the clams, reserving the juice.

Cook the bacon in a frying pan using the medium temperature setting. Stir it occasionally until it's done and crispy. Transfer the cooked bacon to drain on alayer of parchment paper or paper towels. Break it apart into bits.

Chop and add the onion to the drippings. Cook and stir them for four to six minutes or until tender. Mix in the flour, stirring until it's blended. Gradually stirin water and reserved clam juice and continue cooking while stirring until it's bubbly.

Peel, slice, and add potatoes and seasonings, bringing it to a boil, stirring often.Lower the temperature setting and simmer, covered with a lid on the pot until thepotatoes are tender - occasionally stirring (20 to 25 min.).

Pour in the milk, parsley, and clams to heat thoroughly. Top with bacon andserve.

Nutrition: Calories: 63 Fat: 40 g Saturated Fat: 16 g Carbs: 39 g, Fibers: 3 g

Protein: 28 g Sodium: 1281 mg

Hot & Sour Soup: P.F. Chang's Copycat

Preparation Time: 45-50 minutesCooking Time: 20

Servings: 6 - 2 quartsIngredients:

Pork tenderloin (.75 lb.)Olive oil (1 tbsp.)

Sliced mushrooms (.5 lb.) Soy sauce (.25 cup) Chicken broth (6 cups) Chili garlic sauce (2 tbsp.) Black pepper (.75 tsp.) Extra-firm tofu (14 oz. pkg.)

Drained bamboo shoots (8 oz. can)Cornstarch (.3 cup)

White vinegar (.5 cup)Sesame oil (2 tsp.) Water - cold (.3 cup) Green onions (sliced)

Water chestnuts (8 oz. can)Direction

Slice the pork into 1.25-inch by 0.25-inch strips. Drain and cut the tofu into ¼-inch cubes. Drain and slice the water chestnuts.

Prepare a Dutch oven with oil and brown the pork until no longer pink. Transferit from the pan and cover it to keep it warm.

Slice and add the mushrooms sautéing until they are tender. Set aside and keepthem warm.

Add the chili garlic sauce, soy sauce, broth, and pepper to the pan. Wait for it toboil and lower the temperature setting. Put the top on the pot and simmer it for

Alex's Santa Fe Burger

Preparation Time: 15 minutesCooking Time: 15 minutes Servings: 4

Ingredients For Burgers:

12 yellow or blue corn tortilla chips1 poblano Chile, large

4 hamburger buns, split; toasted

1 ½ pounds 80% lean ground chuck or 90% lean ground turkey2 ½ tablespoons canola oil

Freshly ground black pepper & saltFor Queso Sauce:

tablespoon all-purpose flour

cups Monterey Jack cheese, coarsely grated (approximately 8 ounces)1 tablespoon unsalted butter

1 ½ cups whole milk

Freshly ground black pepper & saltDirections

Preheat oven to 375 F.

Remove & place the Chile in alarge bowl; cover using a plastic wrap & let steam for 12 to 15 more minutes. Peel stem & seed the Chile then chop it coarsely.

For Queso Sauce: Heat the butter over medium heat in a small saucepan until completely melted. Add the milk; stir well and increase the heat to high; cook for 3 to 5 minutes, until thickened slightly, whisking constantly.

Evenly divide the meat into 4 portions. Loosely form each portion into a ¾" thick burger & make a deep depression in the middle Cook the burgers in the leftoveroil

Cover with the bun tops; serve immediately & enjoy.

Nutrition: Total fat 14g Carbohydrates 24g Protein 17g Calories 264

Chili's 1975 Soft Tacos

Cooking Time: 12 hours & 15 minutes Servings: 6

Ingredients

1 ½ pounds beef chuck pot roast, fat trimmed 12 corn tortillas (6" each)

5 teaspoons chili powder

2 jars mild or medium tomato-based salsa (16 ounces each) 3 cups fresh lettuce, shredded

avocado

tablespoons cider vinegar

¾ cup sour cream Directions

Spoon a cup of salsa into a small bowl & reserve. Combine the leftover salsa with chili powder and vinegar in a slow cooker. Add beef; cover & cook for 10 to 12 hours on low heat, until the beef shreds easily. Shred the meat, using two forks & spoon into a large-sized serving bowl.

Preheat oven to 300 F. Stack the tortillas, wrap in foil & bake in the preheated oven for 8 to 10 minutes, until warm. Place lettuce and sour cream in bowls. Just before serving; pit, peel & dice the avocado & place in a small bowl. Put out the bowls (including the salsa) & assemble tacos at table.

Nutrition: Calories: 150 Carbohydrates: 10g Fat: 6g Protein: 19g

Shrimp Scampi

Cooking Time: 30 minutes Servings: 4

Ingredients:

1–2 pounds fresh shrimp, cleaned, deveined, and butterflied 1 cup milk3 tablespoons olive oil

½ cup all-purpose flour

4 tablespoons Parmesan cheese, divided

¼ teaspoon salt

½ teaspoon fresh ground black pepper

¼ teaspoon cayenne pepper6–8 whole garlic cloves

5–7 leaves fresh basil, cut into strips 1 diced tomato

tablespoons Parmesan cheese, finely grated 1 shallot, diced

1-pound angel hair pasta, cooked (hot) Parsley, to garnish

Directions:

Put the shrimp in the milk and let it sit.

In a shallow bowl, combine the flour, 2 tablespoons of Parmesan, salt, pepper, and cayenne.

Pour the olive oil in a large skillet, making sure it's enough to cover the bottom.Heat over medium-high heat.

Take the shrimp from the milk and dredge in flour mixture. Transfer it to the skillet and cook about 2 minutes on each side. After the shrimp cooks, transfer itto a plate covered with a paper towel to drain.

(Don't worry about any bits left from the shrimp because these will add flavor and helpto thicken the sauce.)

Add the cream and simmer for about 10 more minutes, then add the basil, tomato, cheese, and shallots. Stir to combine.

Add the shrimp to the skillet and remove it from the heat.

Arrange the pasta on serving plates, topped with shrimp and covered with sauce.Garnish with parsley.

Nutrition: Calories: 454 Fat: 54 g Carbohydrates: 152 g Protein: 41 g Sodium:

1614 mg

Red Beans and Rice from Popeye's

Cooking Time: 40 minutes Servings: 10

Ingredients:

14-ounce cans red beans

¾ pounds smoked ham hock 1¼ cups water

½ teaspoon onion powder

½ teaspoon garlic salt

¼ teaspoon red pepper flakes

½ teaspoon salt

3 tablespoons lard Steamed long-grain rice
Directions:

Add 2 canned red beans, ham hock, and water to pot. Cook on medium heat and let simmer for about 1 hour.

Remove from heat and wait until meat is cool enough to handle. Then, removemeat from bone.

In a food processor, add meat, cooked red beans and water mixture, onion powder, garlic salt, red pepper, salt, and lard. Pulse for 4 seconds. You want thebeans to be cut and the liquid thickened. Drain remaining 1 can red beans and add to food processor. Pulse for only 1 or 2 seconds.

Serve over steamed rice.

Nutrition: Calories: 445Fat: 12 g Saturated fat: 4g Carbohydrates: 67 g Sugar: 1g Fibers: 9 g Protein: 17 g Sodium: 670 mg

Panda Express' Beef and Broccoli

Cooking Time: 15 minutes Servings: 4

Ingredients:

tablespoons cornstarch, divided

tablespoons Chinese rice wine, divided

1-pound flank steak, cut thinly against the grain

1-pound broccoli florets, chopped into small pieces
2 tablespoons oyster sauce

2 tablespoons water

1 tablespoon cornstarch 2 tablespoons canola oil

¼ teaspoon sesame oil

teaspoon

s sesame seedsDirections:

Place beef inside and seal tightly. Massage bag to fully coat beef.

Set aside to marinate for at slightest 20 minutes. Rinse broccoli and put in a nonreactive bowl. Put a damp paper towel on beat, at that point microwave for 2minutes.

Set aside.

Stir oyster sauce, water, 1 tablespoon Chinese rice wine, brown sugar, soy sauce,and remaining cornstarch in a bowl until well mixed. Set aside.

Heat wok over high heat. You want the wok to be very hot. Then, heat canola and sesame oil in wok and wait to become hot. Working in batches, add steak and cook over high heat for 1 minute.

To the same wok, add garlic and ginger. Sauté for about 10 to 15 seconds then return beef to wok. Toss in heated broccoli. Slightly stir prepared sauce to makesure cornstarch is not settled on the bottom, then add to wok. Toss everything insauce to combine. Continue cooking until sauce becomes thick.

Garnish with sesame seeds. Serve.

Nutrition: Calories: 324 Fat: 17 g Saturated fat: 4g Carbohydrates: 13 g Sugar: 6g Fibers: 3 g Protein: 28 g Sodium: 464 mg

Sizzling Steak, Cheese, and Mushrooms Skillet fromApplebee's

Cooking Time: 1 hour and 35 minutesServings: 4

Ingredients:

head garlic, cut crosswise

2 tablespoons butter1 large yellow onion

8 ounces cremini mushroomsSalt and pepper to

taste

½ cup milk

¼ cup cream

3 tablespoons butter

2½ pounds 1-inch thick sirloin steak, cut into 4 large pieces8 slices mozzarella cheese

Directions:

Preheat oven to 300°F.

Position garlic on foil. Pour 1 tablespoon olive oil to the inner sides where the garlic was cut, then wrap foil around garlic.

 Remove from oven and squeeze out garlic from head. Transfer to a bowl or mortar. Add salt and pepper, then mash together. Set aside.

In a pot, add potatoes. Pour enough water on top to cover potatoes. Bring to a boil. Once boiling, reduce heat to medium. Simmer for about 20 to 25 minutes or until potatoes become tender.

Melt butter on a non-stick pan over medium-low heat. Add onions and sauté forabout 15 minutes until a bit tender. Toss in mushrooms and sauté, adjusting heatto medium. Season with salt and pepper. Cook for 10 minutes more. Set aside and keep warm.

Drain potatoes, then mash using an electric mixer on low speed. While mashing,gradually pour in milk, cream, butter, and mashed garlic with olive oil. Keep blending until everything is cream-like and smooth. Remove from mixer and place a cover on top of bowl. Set aside and keep warm.

Evenly coat steak pieces with remaining 1 tablespoon olive oil on all sides.

Heat grill, then place meat on grill. Cook for 4 minutes. Flip and add mozzarellaslices on top. Add additional minutes for increased doneness.

Transfer steaks to serving plates then top with onion/mushroom mixture.Place mashed potatoes on the side. Serve.

Nutrition: Calories: 1159 Fat: 60 g Saturated fat: 29 g Carbohydrates: 47 g

Sugar: 4 g Fibers: 6 g

Protein: 107 g Sodium: 1495 mg

Chili from Steak n' Shake

Cooking Time: 6 minutes Servings: 6

Ingredients:

tablespoon olive oil2 pounds ground beef

½ teaspoon salt

tablespoons onion powder1 tablespoon chili powder

2 teaspoons ground cumin

½ teaspoon ground black pepper2 teaspoons cocoa powder

6 ounces canned tomato paste 13½ ounces canned tomato sauce1 cup Pepsi

27 ounces canned kidney beans

Shredded cheese, sliced green onions for toppings, if desiredDirections:

Heat oil in a pan. Add beef and cook until brown, drain, then remove from heat.

In a bowl, add cooked meat, salt, onion powder, chili powder, cumin, pepper, cocoa powder, tomato paste, tomato sauce, and Pepsi. Mix until combined.

Pour blend into a blender and puree until well mixed. Add blend into moderate cooker. Pour in beans. Cover and set moderate cooker to moo setting and cook for 6 hours

.

Nutrition: Calories: 653Fat: 41 g Saturated fat: 17 g Carbohydrates: 38 g Sugar:12 g Fibers: 11 g

Protein: 35 g Sodium: 1308 mg

about ten minutes. Toss the meat and mushrooms back to the dutch oven. Stir inthe water chestnuts, bamboo shoots, tofu, and vinegar. Simmer it with the lid offof the pot for about ten minutes.

Whisk the cornstarch and water until smooth, and slowly stir it into the soup. Wait for it to boil and continue cooking until it is thickened or about two minutes. Transfer the pan from the hot burner.

Pour in and mix in the sesame oil. Garnish each of the servings with onions.

Nutrition: Calories: 63 Fat: 40 g Saturated Fat: 16 g Carbs: 39 g, Fibers: 3 g

Protein: 28 g Sodium: 1281 mg

CPSIA information can be obtained
at www.ICGtesting.com
Printed in the USA
BVHW091805280621
610633BV00008B/1399

9 781803 213149